Pebble® Plus

Science Builders

Compost Basics

by Mari Schuh

Consulting Editor: Gail Saunders-Smith, PhD

Consultant: Joanne K. Olson, PhD
Associate Professor, Science Education
Center for Excellence in Science & Mathematics Education
Iowa State University, Ames

CAPSTONE PRESS
a capstone imprint

Pebble Plus is published by Capstone Press,
151 Good Counsel Drive, P.O. Box 669, Mankato, Minnesota 56002.
www.capstonepub.com

 Books published by Capstone Press are manufactured with paper containing at least 10 percent post-consumer waste.

Library of Congress Cataloging-in-Publication Data
Schuh, Mari C., 1975–
    Compost basics / by Mari Schuh.
        p. cm.—(Pebble plus. Science builders)
    Summary: "Simple text and full-color photographs provide a brief introduction to compost"—Provided by publisher.
    ISBN 978-1-4296-6073-0 (library binding)
    ISBN 978-1-4296-7106-4 (paperback)
    1. Compost—Juvenile literature. I. Title. II. Series: Pebble plus. Science builders.
    S661.S355 2012
    631.8'75—dc22   2010053931

Editorial Credits
Erika L. Shores, editor; Bobbie Nuytten and Ashlee Suker, designers; Wanda Winch, media researcher;
    Laura Manthe, production specialist

Photo Credits
Alamy: Arco Images/O. Diez, 13, Jim West, 17; Corbis: Macduff Everton, 15; iStockphoto: Stephen Walls, 21;
Photolibrary: Peter Arnold/Matt Meadows, 11, Philippe Giraud, 7; Shutterstock: LianeM, cover, 1, 9, 22, 24, Mikael
Damkier, 5; Visuals Unlimited: Gap Photos/Zara Napier, 19

The author dedicates this book to Ben Johnston-Krase, an avid composter who believes, "The smell of autumn is the smell of creation slowly and graciously returning to the soil, where it will await the day it can energize the next generation of shoots and saplings."

Note to Parents and Teachers

The Science Builders series supports national science standards related to earth science. This book describes and illustrates compost. The images support early readers in understanding the text. The repetition of words and phrases helps early readers learn new words. This book also introduces early readers to subject-specific vocabulary words, which are defined in the Glossary section. Early readers may need assistance to read some words and to use the Table of Contents, Glossary, Read More, Internet Sites, and Index sections of the book.

Printed in the United States of America in North Mankato, Minnesota.

032011   006110CGF11

Table of Contents

What Is Composting?

Leaves gently fall to the ground. Over time, the leaves break down and decay. They slowly turn into nutrients for the soil.

The leaves are now compost.

Compost is decaying plant material.

Composting is how nature

recycles old plants to make

new plants.

Composting in Nature

When a plant dies,

it starts to decay.

Fungi and bacteria break down

the plant into smaller pieces.

The plant pieces slowly turn

into rich soil called humus.

Humus helps new plants grow.

Humus is full of nutrients

that plants need.

Composting at Home

People make compost
using kitchen and yard waste.
Vegetable scraps, leaves,
and grass clippings are
piled together.

Fungi, bacteria, worms,

and other creatures break down

the waste. The compost pile

gets warm and steamy.

Compost piles need to be moist
so fungi and bacteria can grow.
Mixing the compost pile helps
it get enough air.

Most waste decays into compost in less than a year. Then it's added to gardens to make the soil rich and able to hold water.

Composting keeps

plant waste out of landfills.

Compost makes soil just right

for new plants to grow.

Glossary

bacteria—tiny organisms that exist inside and around all living things

decay—to start to go bad, rot, or break down

fungi—a type of organism that survives by taking in nutrients from other living or dead organisms

humus—a dark, rich material full of nutrients from rotting plants and animals

landfill—a place where garbage is dumped and buried

nutrient—a substance needed by a living thing to stay healthy

recycle—to use old items to make new items

waste—something left over and no longer needed; kitchen waste includes scraps of fruits and vegetables; yard waste includes leaves, sticks, and lawn clippings

Read More

Chappell, Rachel. *What's Going on in the Compost Pile? A Book about Systems.* Big Ideas for Young Scientists. Vero Beach, Fla.: Rourke Pub., 2008.

Katz Cooper, Sharon. *The Compost Heap.* Horrible Habitats. Chicago: Raintree, 2010.

Koontz, Robin Michal. *Composting: Nature's Recyclers.* Amazing Science. Minneapolis: Picture Window Books, 2007.

Internet Sites

FactHound offers a safe, fun way to find Internet sites related to this book. All of the sites on FactHound have been researched by our staff.

Here's all you do:

Visit *www.facthound.com*

Type in this code: 9781429660730

Check out projects, games and lots more at
www.capstonekids.com

Index

Word Count: 181

Grade: 1

Early-Intervention Level: 20